Christmas Stocking Pattern
Cute Dog Stocking for Kids

DEDICATION

Contents

19 Best Dog Christmas Stockings for Very Good Boys and Girls

One surefire way to get your pup's tail wagging this Christmas? Present them with their very own Christmas stocking! (And yes, if your pooch doesn't have their own personalized Christmas stocking by now, you're really not celebrating Christmas to its fullest potential.) We rounded up the very best dog Christmas stockings to help you make this day that is so special to humans equally as enjoyable for the furry ones in your life. From customizable stockings that display your four-legged friend's name, to a range of holiday tones and cozy textures, and, more importantly, stockings that are large enough to be stuffed with lots and lots of tail-wagging treats, we've covered every possible stocking idea ! After all, besides the rare chewed high-heel or missing piece of bacon from your Christmas brunch plate, Fido has been good all year long, right?

And while you're shopping for your pup, don't forget to pick out a few things for yourself or gifts for the other dog lovers in your life. We love anything that has to do with our furry friends and we know there are others out there that feel the same way we do! Check out the cutest dog Christmas stockings right here—and don't forget to start brainstorming the best dog gifts too, since those stockings need stuffing, and we're not talking about the white fluffy stuffing the ends up all over your house directly after your dog tries out a new toy.

Simple Dog Christmas Stocking Ideas

Velvet Dog Christmas Stocking Customized Embroidered

Paw prints, soft red velvet, and your pup's name on top check all of our the boxes for the perfect dog Christmas stocking.

Personalized Linen Dog Christmas Stocking

We love the minimalistic look of this burlap and linen stocking that can be personalized with your dog's breed and name.

Simple Dog Christmas Stocking Ideas

Burlap Dog Christmas Stocking

If you're looking for the perfect dog Christmas stocking to match your farmhouse style, this option is the one for you. It's even topped off with a burlap bow!

Paw Print Stocking

Your pup will go mad for plaid once he sees his name on one of these cozy-looking stockings.

Simple Dog Christmas Stocking Ideas

Personalized Dog Bone Christmas Stocking

Fish and bone shapes make for paw-fully adorable stockings—and a bow and name tag just add to the cuteness.

Boston Terrier Christmas Stocking

Simple Dog Christmas Stocking Ideas

You'll love the chic color palette on this stocking almost as much as you love your Boston terrier.

Embroidered Dog Christmas Stocking

Consider this sweet, smiling face an extra incentive for Santa to stuff the stocking with a few extra treats.

Simple Dog Christmas Stocking Ideas

Paw Print Christmas Stocking

Going for a red and white Santa suit-inspired decor vibe? This plush paw stocking works beautifully.

Knit Dog Christmas Stocking

If you're after a cozy and homey vibe this holiday season, this knit dog Christmas stocking is the one for you.

Simple Dog Christmas Stocking Ideas

Embroidered Dog and Cat Christmas Stocking

This cute pet stocking is guaranteed to last for years to come. Plus, you can get a matching one for your feline friend too.

Dog Christmas Stocking With Toys

Simple Dog Christmas Stocking Ideas

Check off your Christmas decorating and shopping lists at the same time with this stocking that comes stuffed with special holiday toys for your canine.

Personalized Burlap Cat and Dog Christmas Stocking

Clocking in at under $20, this burlap beauty comes with personalization options to boot.

Dog Breed Christmas Stocking

Make your furry friend's Christmas feel special without spending a ton of money with this series of dog breed stockings. With more than 50 different types to choose from, you're bound to find one that looks just like your precious pup.

14 OF 19

Handmade Hooked Dog Christmas Stocking

Simple Dog Christmas Stocking Ideas

Get the look and feel of grandma's handiwork with this handmade knit Christmas stocking.

15 OF 19

Dog Bone Christmas Stocking

Simple Dog Christmas Stocking Ideas

Throw your fur baby a bone—preferably a big one like this—but don't forget to fill with plenty of edible Christmas biscuits and bones too.

Personalized Paw Christmas Stockings for Dogs

Pamper your pooch with special surprises hidden inside a personalized, paw-shaped Christmas stocking.

Ruffled Dog Christmas Stocking

Simple Dog Christmas Stocking Ideas

This Christmas dog stocking has a touch of country chic to it

Personalized Pet Stocking

How adorable are these Santa-themed dog Christmas stockings?!

Simple Dog Christmas Stocking Ideas

Quilted Dog Bone Christmas Stocking

If the color palette for your Christmas decorations includes mostly neutrals, this dog stocking will fit right in.

Diy Dog Christmas Stocking

This shop has been compensated by Collective Bias, Inc. and its advertiser. All opinions are mine alone. #ClausAndPaws #CollectiveBias

Furry babies are the best.

Unlike preteen boys, they don't leave dirty socks all over the house or roll their eyes at Etta James in carline. Pets give unconditional love. No matter what.

Give your pets a little extra love this holiday season with DIY Dog Christmas Stocking filled with yummy pet treats . Keep reading for step-by-step directions to create a stocking for your dog or cat.

Simple Dog Christmas Stocking Ideas

Our family has a sweet yellow dog named Barley and a feisty grey kitty named Thunder. As you can see, they love each other and often sleep curled together on our back deck. The children have grown up with these furry babies and we all love them dearly.

At Christmas I usually hang up a plain felt stocking for the pets. But this year we are taking the plain stocking one step further with felt embellishments and ribbon. It's a no-sew stocking that anyone could make!

Simple Dog Christmas Stocking Ideas

DIY DOG CHRISTMAS STOCKING ~ SUPPLIES

- Pre-Made Felt Stocking
- Felt Sheets
- Ribbon
- Pet Silhouettes

Instead of sewing my own pet stockings, I purchased a pre-made stocking from my favorite craft store. They were less than $2 each (50% off) and are so very cute!

Simple Dog Christmas Stocking Ideas

When I get ready to work on a project I like to gather all the materials I think I may need. Even if I don't use everything all the different patterns and colors spark my creativity!

Next I searched online for a dog and cat silhouette I loved. Here's where this personalized stocking project is going to get really low-tech: since our printer is kaput I actually held a piece of paper on the computer screen and traced each silhouette.

Simple Dog Christmas Stocking Ideas

Pin the silhouettes to the felt (thicker felt works better) then cut using sharp scissors. The children wanted Thunder the cat to be grey and I chose black for Barley the dog.

Simple Dog Christmas Stocking Ideas

Secure the grey felt kitty to the stocking with hot glue. A handsome ribbon bow gives the Christmas stocking for the cat a dashing personality.

Simple Dog Christmas Stocking Ideas

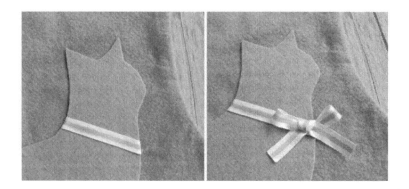

The DIY Dog Christmas Stocking was made the same way. Barley got a frilly girly ribbon collar and a perky bow on top of her head.

Just look at how sweet that red bow is! Love it!

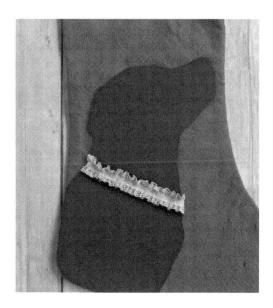

Simple Dog Christmas Stocking Ideas

To make the pet stockings personalized, I used the same technique as the silhouettes to cut out initials for Barley and Thunder's stocking. Secure the letters with hot glue.

Simple Dog Christmas Stocking Ideas

Now that the personalized Christmas stockings are finished, I'm off to Walmart to find a yummies for our pets. A few items for stocking stuffers and a couple of things for under the Christmas tree is what I'm searching for.

Simple Dog Christmas Stocking Ideas

Be sure to check out more great gift ideas for pets. (Love those funny Santa hats and reindeer antlers!) What kind of treats do your fur babies love?

Pattern for A Cute Personalized Dog Christmas Stocking

HOW TO MAKE A CUTE PERSONALIZED DOG CHRISTMAS STOCKING

I say that is is a personalized dog Christmas stocking, just because I made it for our beloved dog Toby. But you could use this pattern to make this Christmas stocking for any pet with paws such as a cat!

I work from home and often the only company I have for the whole day is our rescue dog, Toby. Every day Toby and I start the day with a morning dog walk and a coffee in the park. Toby then sticks to my side for the rest of the day. He even manages to get himself into some of my craft photos.

This year whilst crafting for Christmas I decided to make something for Toby as well. As a family, we love to give Toby a few extra treats at Christmas and this personalized doggy Christmas stocking is perfect for that.

Simple Dog Christmas Stocking Ideas

This pet Christmas stocking isn't the only thing I've crafted for Toby. In the past I've made him some cute denim handmade dog toys before.

Simple Dog Christmas Stocking Ideas

WHAT YOU NEED TO MAKE A PERSONALIZED DOG CHRISTMAS STOCKING

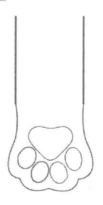

- Burlap, hessian, jute, sacking or whatever you call it!

Simple Dog Christmas Stocking Ideas

- Red fabric for the top and paw pads. I had an old pair of red jeans and used this for the top but any red fabric would do. I also had some scrap red leather I used for the paw pads. However, you could just as easily use red felt.

- Needle and thread

- Fabric glue

- Letter stencils and white paint

Simple Dog Christmas Stocking Ideas

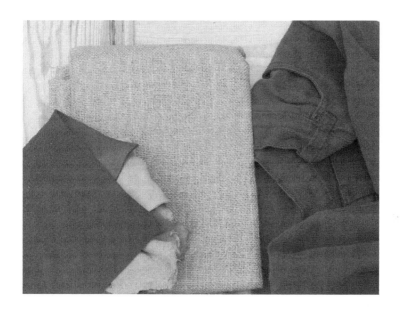

1. Print out the dog paw pattern. I printed out the paw pattern onto A3 paper. If you don't have an A3 printer your local copy shop should be able to enlarge and print the pattern for you. Or you could try drawing your own pattern onto A3 paper freehand.

2. Cut out the paw stocking pattern and place ontop of the burlap/hessian. I doubled over the hessian so that I could cut out 2 paws at the same time. Draw around the paw pattern with a sharpie and then cut it out.

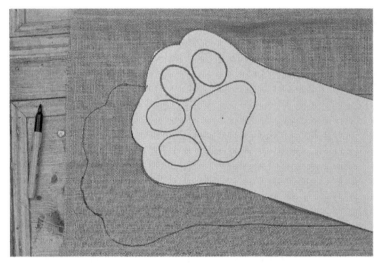

3. Next sew both the cut out paws together leaving a margin of about 5mm. If you don't have a sewing machine, burlap is very easy to sew by hand.

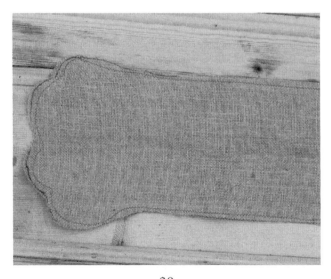

4. Turn the stitched paw inside out so that the stitching is on the inside. For the cuff I used the bottom of a pair of red jeans which I stitched to the top of the dog Christmas stocking. If you don't have a pair of old red jeans just use some other red fabric such as felt. The cuff was about 9cm long.

5. Next cut out the paw pads from the Christmas stocking pattern and use them as a template. Draw around the pad templates on your chosen red fabric and cut out the pads. I used scrap leather for this but craft felt will work just as well.

Simple Dog Christmas Stocking Ideas

6. Using a fabric glue stick the paw pads onto the front of the dog Christmas stocking.

7. Stitch on a loop for hanging the stocking on the edge of the cuff. I used a belt loop from the jeans.

8. Finish off the pet Christmas stocking by personalizing it. For this I stenciled on Toby's name in white on the red cuff.

All that is left to do now is to fill and hang the stocking. I know Toby won't really know whether or not he had a stocking but he will enjoy the treats inside. Also as a loved member of the family he deserves to have his own personalized dog Christmas stocking.

Christmas Stocking Pattern

Christmas stocking pattern – Use this free stocking pattern to make the best diy Christmas stockings for the entire family. Also, they are reversible, so you'll be able to match them to your Christmas decor for years to come! No-fold cuff, making sure you use the least fabric you need for a polished look. No gaping, and a well-designed pattern for an easy sewing process. Check it out!

This post may contain affiliate links. Thanks for your support. Christmas sewing, anyone? Yes! There are tons of Christmas sewing projects on this blog. Feel free to check them all out, including these ideas:

- 37 Pretty DIY Holiday Decorations to Sew!
- Quick DIY Gift Bag – In Minutes!
- Quilted Christmas Tree Skirt – What I made!
- 15+ Cutest Diy Christmas Gifts For Kids

Now back to sewing Christmas stockings. The diy stocking pattern is available from my shop – but WAIT! Get it for FREE with 100% OFF code for all my newsletter subscribers! (new subscribers can join here, existing subscribers: see my latest newsletter) Read on to find out more.

GOOD DESIGN + LESS FABRIC + REVERSIBLE STOCKING

I made this tutorial a bit different from the usual stocking tutorials, to make it even easier, and it's also a bit because I'm always looking for the most efficient way to use less fabric — with the same, or even better visual effect. Check out how the no-fold cuff is constructed — easier and faster to sew, using up less fabric than other same-sized stockings with cuffs folded back.

Save this project for later to Pinterest using THIS LINK or the image below, so you remember how to use your pattern:

You only need two fat quarters of fabric, and scrap pieces for the cuff. If you use fat quarters with pretty Christmas prints, your diy Christmas stocking will be reversible!

I used these colorful Christmas prints from the Merry And Bright collection designed by @echoparkpaper for Riley Blake Designs:

I loved the classic colors and those cute vintage Christmas illustrations – oh, and the gift boxes and the green ornaments were my favorites! Also, mixing large and small prints made it easy for me to include them into all kinds of Christmas sewing projects. – Get my entire Handmade Holidays collection of patterns and templates here. (Free, no code required.)

Simple Dog Christmas Stocking Ideas

Or check out what else I've made with these prints – origami ornaments and this free gift card holder pattern.

If you want to see what other crafty little Christmas sewing projects I'll post with these prints, make sure to sign up for the free weekly newsletter (here), so you don't miss out on them!

FINISHED SIZE OF THESE DIY CHRISTMAS STOCKINGS
Height 13" (33 cm), width of the top opening 6" (15 cm)

HOW MUCH FABRIC DO I NEED TO MAKE A CHRISTMAS STOCKING?
Usually, half a yard (half a meter) will be more than enough to make one Christmas stocking in average size, but it's even more fun if you use scraps.

DIY CHRISTMAS STOCKING SUPPLIES

Simple Dog Christmas Stocking Ideas

- two fat quarters of quilting fabric (I used prints from the Merry And Bright collection)

- a fat eighth of accent or solid fabric

- two scrap pieces of fusible fleece for the cuff

- optional: use fusible fleece for the entire outer stocking if you want a stable stocking that will stand up on its own or propped against the wall.

- sewing machine or needle, pins or sewing clips,

- iron, scissors, or rotary cutter plus cutting mat (I use this one by Olfa)

- the PDF Pattern file — that's available to all my newsletter subscribers with an exclusive 100% OFF code for free. You get once you've confirmed your subscription (new subscribers: join here, existing subscribers: enter SHOP here and use 100%off coupon from my latest newsletter)

If you don't want to sign up for my newsletter, you can still purchase the pattern in the shop here.

CHRISTMAS STOCKING WITH CUFF – TUTORIAL

Now, first for those who love watching videos, I've made a little slideshow-style video to outline the sewing process — sit back, watch and relax:

Now on to the written step-by-step directions:

HOW TO CUT THE FABRIC FOR CHRISTMAS STOCKING

Simple Dog Christmas Stocking Ideas

1) After you've printed the free PDF template (see below) to a piece of cardboard or paper, cut the cuffs from pattern piece No2 – cut on fold, as indicated on the pattern piece. Then cut out two smaller pieces from fusible fleece to reinforce the stocking, so it will retain the form when hanging from your mantelpiece.

2) Fuse the fleece to the back of the cuff fabric.

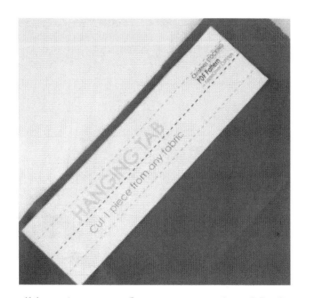

3) Cut the small hanging strap from pattern piece No 3.

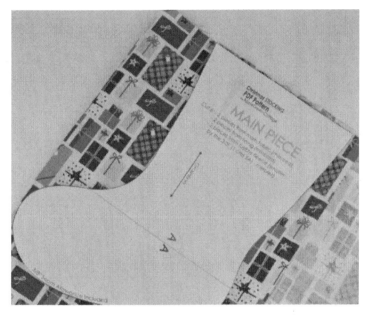

4) Cut the main stocking pieces (pattern piece No 1).

NOTE: First fold the fabric wrong sides together and place pattern piece No1 on it. Cut 2 pieces, they will be mirrored. This is important. Repeat to cut 2 main stocking pieces from lining – these two pieces should be mirror images of each other, too.

The fusible fleece layer is optional. These are the pieces you have now:

Simple Dog Christmas Stocking Ideas

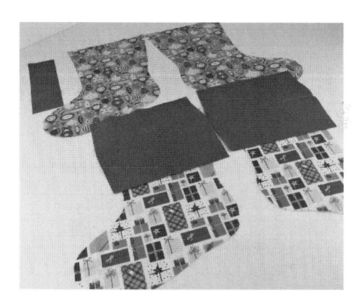

5) Arrange the pieces like this, to make the assembly super easy:

Simple Dog Christmas Stocking Ideas

HOW TO STITCH THE PIECES TOGETHER

6) Place one of the main outer piece on a flat surface and place the cuff on it, so the right sides will be together and the interfaced cuff

edge is aligned with the top edge of the main outer piece. Stitch using a 3/8" (1 cm) seam allowance.

7) Place the remaining edge of the cuff right side up and place the upper edge of the main lining piece right side-down. Stitch, using the 3/8" (1 cm) seam allowance, again leaving a gap for turning.

8) Repeat with the other set of pieces, so this is what you have now:

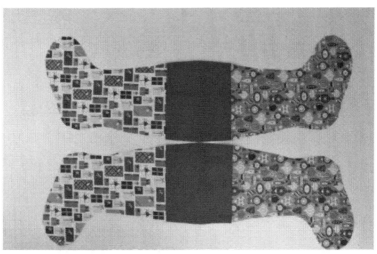

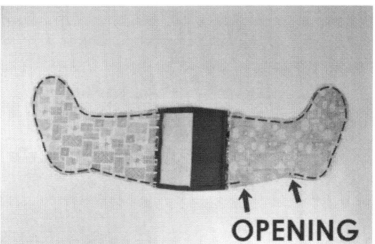

OPENING

9) Place the pieces right-sides-together and sew around, using a 3/8" (1 cm) seam allowance. Make sure to leave an opening for turning on the back seam of the lining piece.

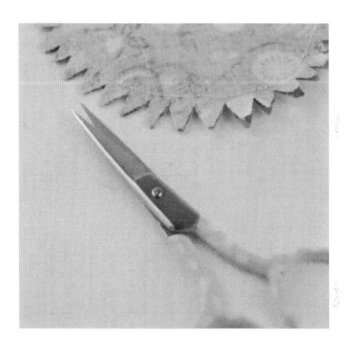

10) Clip the concave curves and notch the 'hills', taking care not to snip into stitches.

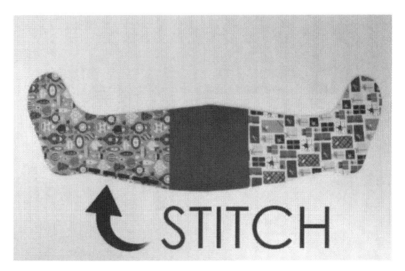

11) Turn right side out, press and tuck the lining in.

ATTACH THE HANGING TAB

The only piece left is the 7" by 2" tab – once finished, it will turn into a 3" long loop. Feel free to adjust to the size you need.

12) Fold along the long edges, first along the center, then unfold and press the sides towards the center. Refold along the original center and press. I finished the ends and topstitched on both long edges, and got this:

Simple Dog Christmas Stocking Ideas

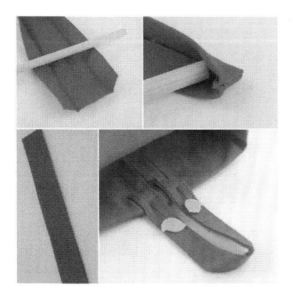

13) Pin the two ends on the inner side of the cuff, very close to the back center seam, like this:

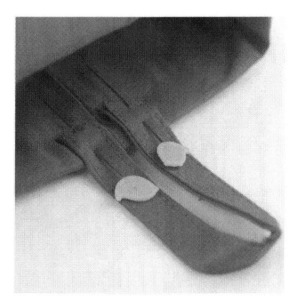

14) Stitch, back- and forth a few times to secure the seam. Finished.

Simple Dog Christmas Stocking Ideas

It's easy and quick!

I hope this makes it super easy for you to sew your own set of beautiful Christmas stockings for the entire family, to last for years to come! Since they are reversible, you'll be able to mix and match, and to change the look of your Christmas decor just by flipping the lining right side out. Enjoy! Also, check out my 6-sized Christmas gift bag pattern here in my shop. For all your handmade presents!

Easy DIY Christmas Stockings

This is not the first time I have made DIY Christmas stockings. But the last time, I was making them for my family it said, "Mom, Dad, Deb and Deneen" so it was a few years ago 😊 I still have mine, and maybe my sister does too. Sage doesn't care she just thinks it tastes good.

This tastes good, but it would be better if it had cookies in it.

Over the last few years, I have been looking for stockings that I like enough to buy for the whole family And by the family I mean Greg – the boyfriend, Sage -the dog, Angus – the cat, and Me… the boss

Simple Dog Christmas Stocking Ideas

I managed to find a pretty cool kitty stocking for Angus, back in the days when we still had Zellers (All you Canadians will remember my favourite long lost department store)…sniff.

I wanted my stocking to be bright white, clean and simple! I think I achieved it

PS – Click here to see the post for the buffet that the stocking is hanging on

Here is how you can make these too!
Supplies
These are my estimates for supplies: per stocking:

- fabric – 22" x 22"
- fur trim – 22"
- edging trim -45"
- Iron-on Letters (dependent on names)
- thread

Don't worry about a pattern, just use a stocking that you like the shape of, and use this as your template. I used this one:

You could just trace around the stocking, but I made a template from newsprint, because I wanted to make the toe a little rounder. If you want a template for your stocking go to my Member's lounge, and use the one I have there, under the cat stocking pattern.

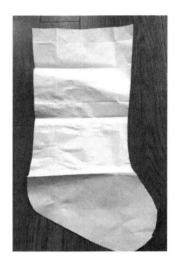

You can use whatever type and colour/pattern of fabric that you want! They don't have to be white like mine. I prefer using quilted fabric, it's easier to work with and the stockings hold their shape

Simple Dog Christmas Stocking Ideas

when they are hanging off of the mantle. If you decide to use silky or lacy fabric, I would suggest attaching it to a backing fabric first. Just lay it over one piece and edge stitch them together, before putting the front and back of the stocking together. It will help to keep it's shape, and make it much easier to work with.

Use tailor's chalk to trace the shapes out on your fabric. This way if you make a mistake it will just brush off.

Trace the outline of the stockings onto your fabric and then just fold it over to get both sides of your DIY Christmas stocking. Pin it inside the chalk lines. Cut through all thicknesses to get both sides of your stocking. You will need sharp scissors! If this doesn't work well, just trace more shapes and cut them out singly.

Simple Dog Christmas Stocking Ideas

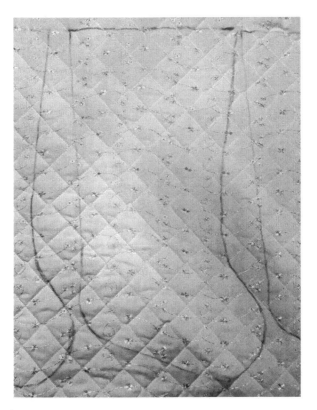

Personalization

Before sewing anything together, put the letters onto the stockings. If you have a sewing machine that does embroidery, you can just embroider your names onto the stockings. But if you don't, then just use iron on letters like I did. This is easy and they look good. Plus you can get them with glitter or rhinestones! Yes!

When shopping for your letters, spell out all of the names you will be

doing, and count out the letters

If you have names with a lot of the same letter, you might need to take this into account when picking letters, as some of them have more of one letter than others. for example we needed 4 g's, and some of the letters only had 1 in each pack, so that would require 4 packages. The ones that I chose had 2 g"s, so it only required 2 packages. But hey, if you have your heart set on specific letters, just go for it. We are building family heirlooms here

I just used my tailor's chalk to draw a line down 6' down from the top of the stocking. Put your fur trim up to see where it comes to, and then decide where you want your names to go.

The letters that I used were iron on "Transfermations" I bought them at Michael's. They worked very well. Just follow the instructions on the package. They are a bit "grippy" so once you get them into place, I just placed the cardboard from the package on top of them and pushed on it, to stick them down a bit before ironing. Also, since you will be using a pressing cloth, just tack them lightly to start, and double check the alignment before securing them firmly.

You can use whatever type of letters works for your aesthetic Here are some options.

Sewing

Time to sew our DIY Christmas stockings!! No inside out sewing for these stockings. Just lay them wrong sides together, right sides out and use an edge stitch to sew them together. This will help to keep the bulk down when you are adding your trim.

Simple Dog Christmas Stocking Ideas

Trials and Tribulations

I had my fair share of first world problems this week. My go to fabric store – Fabricland, was closed for renovations. So, I waited a week for it to re-open. Then when it did, it had a 75% off sale!!! and I left with a spool of thread... Never fails. Then 2 days later, my 30 year old Janome sewing machine finally packed it in. That puppy was a work horse!! This is very similar to my new sewing machine.

Next step is to sew on the trim. Make sure that you buy Double Fold Bias Tape or similar edging that has a finished edge.

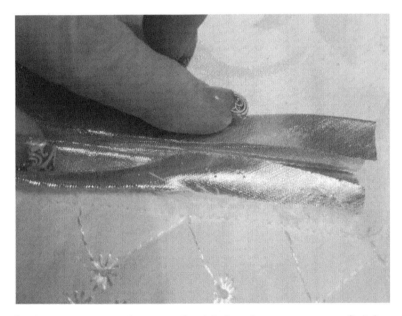

You don't want to muck around with ironing over seam finishes. Just fold the edging over the edge and sew whatever stitch makes you happy I went with a version of a scallop stitch like this:

Simple Dog Christmas Stocking Ideas

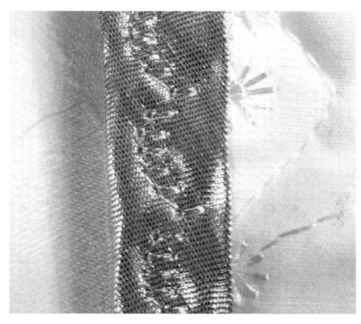

Just keep working your way around the stocking in one continuous piece. Once you get to the end keep using your fancy stitch for another 1-3 inches, and then fold this over to make a loop to hang the stocking by.

Fur it up

I should probably get my cat to help out here. He is very good at furring things up. For that matter so is the dog! The last piece is to add the fur trim. measure the diameter of the top of the stocking and add about 1/2' for seam allowances. Sew the fur right sides together, and push the fur in so it isn't "caught" in the seam. Then turn right side out, and pin it to the top edge of the stocking. Use matching thread and an edge stitch to attach it to the stocking.

You will need to sew it "flat: where the seam binding is. It will not look right if you fold the seam allowance on the edge of the stocking over.

Simple Dog Christmas Stocking Ideas

Now go ahead and personalize these DIY Christmas stockings for your family.

If you are looking for a cat specific. stocking, check out these really cute DIY Stockings for your cat, or your favourite cat person:)

DIY Christmas Stockings – No Sew

Making our own Christmas stockings has really been fun and the kids love pulling out their special stockings when we set up the tree.

These stockings are easy to make! Let me show you how

Supplies for making DIY Christmas Stockings:

- Felt. Lots of felt in all sorts of colors that you want to use.
- Sharp scissors
- Hot glue gun and sticks
- Various embellishments such as sparkly pom poms, small beads, ribbons, yarn, googly eyes, normal pom poms etc.

First you need to decide what size your stocking is going to be then make it a bit bigger to allow for the seams you will be glueing. Cut it in a boot shape.

Simple Dog Christmas Stocking Ideas

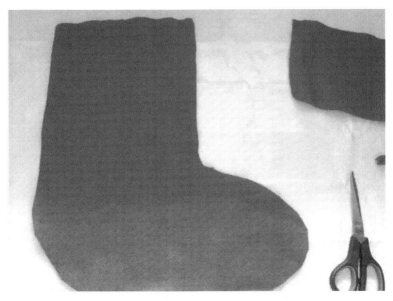

Hot glue the stocking together section by section because hot glue gets cold very fast so it is better to do a bit at a time.

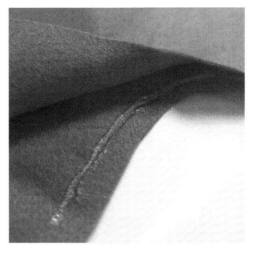

Make all your stockings you aim to make and turn them the right way around when the glue is set.

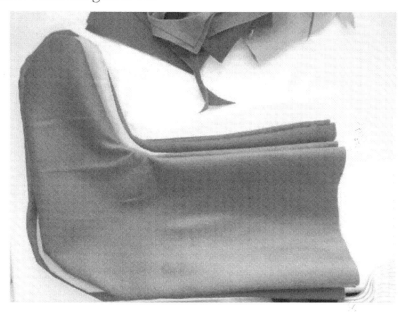

Now there are a few trimmings you can add to these stockings. First is the white rimed stocking. Turn your stocking inside out. Cut a a strip of white felt for the trimming, bigger then the circumference of the stocking. Hot glue it at the top seam all around. Trim the excess white felt and then hot glue it down the side over lapping the two edges.

Simple Dog Christmas Stocking Ideas

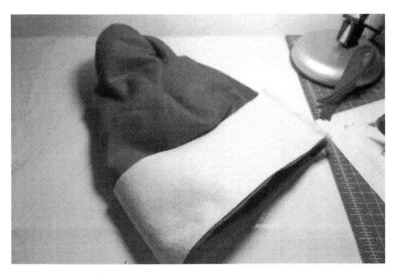

(I took these after decorating to better demonstrate)

As shown in the image below you can see the seam of the joining.

Turn your stocking the right way around and add the hanging tag. It is simply a thin band of felt folded in on itself and hot glued down.

Press the seams down to make it stay neat. I run my hands over them a few times and it seems to do the trick.

Now for the decorating! For the names on the stockings open a word document of any other program that allows you to type and print from. Select a bold font such as impact and type in caps the name for your stocking. Make sure to fill the page with the font size!

I use a glue stick to temporarily hold the paper to the felt while I cut so it doesn't slide around.

Hot glue the name to your stocking once you have positioned it in a place you like.

Simple Dog Christmas Stocking Ideas

Decorating the stocking is totally up to you! On the red stocking I made a snowman. I free hand cut the 2 circles for the body and a hat. The snow is white pom poms and the accessories are bits of various felt. The eyes are googly eyes. These are all hot glued down.

(We had a littler of kittens that year, the poor tree)

I have shared my templates for the other stockings which I made to cut them out myself. They exclude the snowman which I free hand cut.

Printed by Amazon Italia Logistica S.r.l.
Torrazza Piemonte (TO), Italy

62067554R00045